Nobody but You, Lord

Lorena Burnett & The Gift of God Ministries

Galatians 5:22 Love is just like you

AuthorHouse™
1663 Liberty Drive
Bloomington, IN 47403
www.authorhouse.com
Phone: 833-262-8899

Because of the dynamic nature of the Internet, any web addresses or links contained in this book may have changed since publication and may no longer be valid. The views expressed in this work are solely those of the author and do not necessarily reflect the views of the publisher, and the publisher hereby disclaims any responsibility for them.

This book is printed on acid-free paper.

ISBN: 978-1-4389-7696-9 (sc)

Print information available on the last page.

Published by AuthorHouse 08/11/2023

authorHOUSE®

Drawings for *Nobody but You, Lord*

Pick your Dress two dresses on bed has woman and child
I love to play the Game woman and child at the kitchen table
Feeling special on my fourth birthday in the kitchen giving cookies
Momma I'm sick child eating cherries from the tree
Momma I'm sick child with bag boy walking on side walk
Walking with Momma child and woman walking cat by fence
Lonely Days child asleep nun by bed side
The Promise child in bed biting her fingernails
Waving to my brothers and sister child in blue on register waving
Miraculous Healing shadow Of People child wearing white
My first real Fight child fighting background of people
Come and See Two angels in a circle wings are brown & white
The power Of the Trigger child with gun on forehead
The old fashion extension Cord woman with strap child on floor
The iron black iron woman and child brown door
My life flashing before me hospital building, raining, and automobile
Not lucky but blessed by Jesus portrait of woman finger bandage
Healed Of asthma church scene three women
The Angelic Messenger angel with woman
The burning ball of flame man in flame
The demon black door with red fire, brown hand bottom of page
Zorias man with sword

This autobiography is dedicated to the hearing impaired and deaf. This is a personal testimony of Lorena Burnett and The Gift of God Ministries. Jesus, our Lord and Savior can and will use all who are willing to yield their hearts to him. I am a living witness that you can be whatever you desire if you put God first and let his Holy Spirit lead and guide you through all of your trials and tribulations in this world, as well as all of your disappointments. I can truly say, "Nobody but you, Lord, makes me feel the way I do."

This book is also dedicated to my elect grandchildren:
Apryl-Christopher, Amy'ah, Ky'lahn
Michael-Jazmine, Ashlyn, Mikiyah, Tori, Mi'shayla.
Shytia-My'Iahn.

And to my godchildren, Britney, Felicha, Antoinette, Shyneia, and Michael.

In loving Memory of my parents

Mary Ann Rhodes Goodman
April 2, 1918–March 31, 1987
James Ruff Goodman
March 7, 1912–November 2, 1970
Vernon Samuel Goodman
October 6, 1916–February 23.1995

Also for Uncle Edward Rhodes, who always took us riding in his truck and car, gave us money at home at the movies, and took us to the watermelon patch to pick our own watermelon. I miss you, and you will always be in my heart.

For Aunt Dora Lee Rhodes Johnson, whom Mom says I am like. She was a dedicated woman of God. I love and miss you!

And for Aunt Cora Louise Rhodes White, who encouraged me through all of my trials. I miss and love you! The things you instilled in my heart shall never die.

Contents

Preface

As soon as God entrusted me to tell my life story, this book poured out of me. This book is not only about me, but about how God's purpose takes place in our lives. Nothing ever happens by fate. Jesus can bring you from a life of nothing and mold your life into something beautiful. There *is* a purpose for your life.

This book will show you how God can and will deliver you from your pains and wounds. You may not understand things when they are happening to you, but as time goes on, you will. This book also addresses how you will reap in due season if you faint not.

I could not have gone through this life without God's love, grace, and mercy. He has never left us nor forsaken us. I love him from the depth of my being. He loves each one of us in a special way, and he knows what we need and how to give it. It is to His glory that we were born to serve only Him. He places His will in us so we can act according to his good pleasure. Now is the time to submit to Him and become jewels of honor. I pray this book will inspire you to become a servant of Jesus Christ. Amen!

Acknowledgments

I am sending my special thanks and love to Jesus for picking me out of the field of sin and for molding me in His unique fashion and for dispatching His angels to sing to me in every trial I encountered.

I am thankful for the seeds that were planted, watered, and have blossomed into a beautiful flower garden—my children. I am also grateful to Royce Jr., Brittany, Donna, and Chea; Mark, Dervon, his wife, Lisa, Dervon Jr., and Chani; James Terez, his wife, Linda, Kay'in, Naomi, Marlon, and Elijah; Aaron and Erica for all of their tender love, support, and encouragement through the year.

Special love for the beautiful roses, including my niece Marjorie Ann, her husband Willie, her daughter, Dionne Marie, and her son-in-law Jivon; Kindo, Diondrea, Jivona, my niece Alicia De'Nele, Jasmine, Leroy, Jeremy, Marsha; and my nephew, James Neal.

March 29, 1995
Wednesday

The Holy Ghost said to tell you, honey, that there's a mighty breakthrough coming for you in every area of your life. And this breakthrough will not tarry, saith the Lord. For I've given thee a mighty vision, and I shall fulfill my purpose in your life. For yea, even thy voice shall be anointed, anointed, anointed, that as you go forth, saith the Lord thy God, you shall see as the Spirit of God begins to stir your heart, and man's heart shall be stirred as God stirs yours, saith the Lord. Get ready, my child, for a great and mighty breakthrough is coming to you in ministry. For yea, that which you struggled over you will struggle over no more, saith the Lord. For this night the bondages have been broken. This night, saith the Lord, the operations of the enemy have ceased, and yea, I have put a stop to the works of the enemy in your life. Get ready for a mighty breakthrough that is about to take place upon thee. God shall even give thee a change of direction, and He shall set thee where He wants thee, and God shall set thy foot as hinds' feet, and He shall set thy feet upon a rock. Yes, saith the Lord, for you are planted and grounded in me. Get ready for a mighty breakthrough for yea, even this night my Spirit is upon thee. I have called you in the palm of my hand; get ready for a mighty breakthrough, saith the Spirit of God.

Messenger: Brother from Jamaica.

Prologue

Daddy! Daddy, where are you? Come and get me; she is beating me, and she says she is going to kill me. Daddy, where are you? If he only knew where I was, he would come and get me. I am his only child. Although I don't know him, I love him and he loves me. Why won't she tell me his name? Where is he? I want to find him and tell him I want to live with him. She says he is dead, but I know he is not. Daddy! Daddy, where are you?

Lorena didn't know that he knew all the time where she was.

Chapter 1

Early Childhood and Growing Up

My first memory of my sister Faye-Baby is from when she was three years old and I was four. We lived in a two-story white house on Main Street, but we occupied the basement, which consisted of a coal bin. We were in the driveway playing in our separate space, building a sandcastle, except instead of sand, it was rocks and dirt. For some reason Faye-Baby decided to pick up her rock-castle and throw it at me. I then picked up my rock-castle and threw it at her. The dirt and rocks went into her eyes, causing her to scream in pain. I didn't care about her crying; I kept throwing rocks and dirt at her until I heard a loud voice calling my name and telling me to stop. I then realized it was Ms. Lucy, the neighbor across the street. Unbeknownst to me, she told Momma the deed I had done.

Later that day when things were settled and I had forgotten about the fight and Ms. Lucy, Momma called me into the house. She had a limb of a tree in her hand, which we called a switch. She asked no questions. She bluntly told me she was giving me a switching because I could have put my sister's eye out and that I was not to play with the rocks and dirt anymore. I couldn't understand why Faye-Baby didn't get a switching.

The Night before Christmas

The night before Christmas I woke up in the middle of the night excited because I couldn't help thinking about the presents I would receive from Santa Claus. My older sister Marie was cleaning the living room. Through my sleepy eyes, I saw her put something in a Kroger sack. She didn't notice me when I pulled all of the clothes out of the sack. That is when I saw the beautiful doll, Lila Lou. I was so excited I said to my sister, "Look! Look what Santa Claus left me!" My sister snatched the doll from me and told me I didn't see anything and ordered me to go back to bed. If I didn't, Santa Claus wouldn't

come down the chimney and I wouldn't get anything for Christmas. She told me she was going to tell Momma I had gotten out of bed too early, and Momma was going to punish me. So I went back to bed and went to sleep, dreaming about the Lila Lou doll I saw in the Kroger sack.

Christmas Day

I woke early in the morning on Christmas Day very excited. I ran into the living room, and under the Christmas tree were two dolls: Lila Lou and Ragged. I pick up Lila Lou—it had to be my doll! Later that morning my sister Faye-Baby climbed out of bed. There was only one doll left under the tree. "Look at my dolly!" she said to me.

We were both happily playing with our dolls when Momma came into the living room. She glanced at me, and she snatched the doll from my hands saying, "This is not your doll! This is Faye-Baby's dolly. Your doll is Ragged." She then traded dolls between us. I was real mad and threw Ragged across the room screaming, "I don't like that doll!" Momma smiled and simply walked out of the room. Faye-Baby picked up Ragged and said to me, "I like Ragged." She traded dolls, giving me Lila Lou. Momma came back in the room and saw we had switched dolls again. She was angry and traded the dolls once more, giving me Ragged. I didn't play with her. I cried and cried because I wanted Lila Lou.

Pick Your Dress

Momma called me into her bedroom, where I saw there were two dresses lying on the bed. She asked me which dress did I want: the red one or the blue one? I was so excited that she was allowing me to choose the dress I wanted. "The red one!" I said.

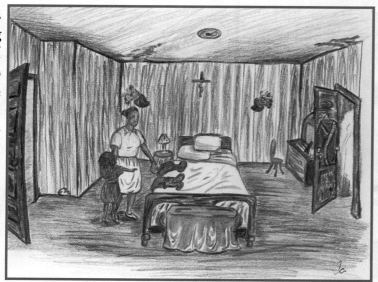

She then answered, "No! That is your sister Faye-Baby's dress. The blue one is yours."

I became very angry. If only she would have said the blue dress was mine, it would have been fine. She gave me a choice, and that hurt the most.

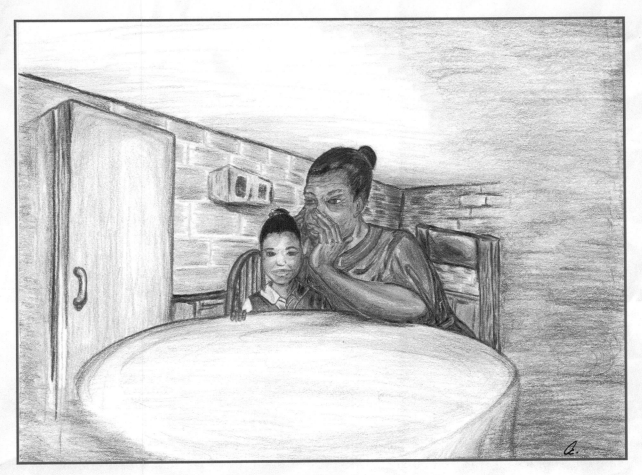

The Game

Momma often called me into the kitchen. She would pick me up and stand me on a chair, and she would play a game with me. I loved to play this game. She would cover my left ear with her hand and whisper in my right ear and then ask, "What did I say?" I didn't hear her words, just her breathing, and it tickled my ear. I would laugh, and Momma would laugh, too. Then she would cover my right ear with her hand and whisper in my left ear, asking me again, "What did I say?" Some of the time I could understand what she said. It would be "What is your name?" or "How old are you?" or something similar. She played this game with me because I was born hearing impaired and my right ear was deformed.

Feeling Special on My Fourth Birthday

I remember other incidents while growing up. I remember one day so vividly because Momma was passing out cookies on this particular day. She called me into the kitchen, where chocolate cookies were on the table. She then gave each of my sisters and brothers one cookie. She told me to hold out both of my hands. She put a cookie in each hand and said, "Lorene, today is April 21, your birthday. You are four years old." I was so thrilled. I jumped up and down because I felt special.

Beginning First Grade

When I was five years old, I didn't attend kindergarten because Momma was afraid the teachers would notice my hearing disability and label me. She didn't understand that I just couldn't distinguish all the sounds of words. I began first grade at Dunbar School when I was six years old. I was a very quiet child. This was because when I talked, I hollered because of my hearing disability. My friends and playmates would often ask me why I talked so loud. I couldn't answer them because I didn't realize I talked loud. Momma's friends and neighbors would also ask the same question. She would tell them I was hard of hearing. So as a small child, I seldom talked because it made me feel sad when people said I talked too loud.

As I grew older, I pretended it didn't bother me. I would shrug off their words and keep talking. I used to think people didn't speak clearly because I couldn't understand their words. Eventually I realized it was me all along who didn't hear clearly.

The Pointer Stick

I will never forget my third grade teacher. She was teaching the class the multiplication tables. She had written them on the chalkboard, and she kept her pointer stick in her hand the whole time. If we didn't recite our tables correctly, she would whack our fingers with the stick. That was our punishment for not knowing. This time she picked me out; she beat the stick on my desk and said "Two times two equals what? Two times three equals what?" I knew the answers but was afraid to talk because of the loudness of my voice. I just stared at her and said nothing. The teacher became really angry. She then took the pointing stick and banged it on my desk again. I moved my hand in time, and the stick broke. Fear gripped my heart, and I never did grow to like that teacher.

Chapter 2

Walking to Church with Momma

At the age of five I usually walked to church with Momma. I loved Sunday school; sometimes Momma didn't go to Sunday school and would come later to worship service. That is when I would walk to church by myself. Momma always gave me pennies or a button to place in the offering basket. At some point the deacons would take their hats off to pass around, and we put the money or button in the hats. Then they would bless the donation and recite these words: Put a penny in the old man's hat. If you haven't got a penny, a button will do; if you haven't got a button, then God bless you. I asked Momma what this saying meant. Momma taught us church values. She said to always save 10 percent of your money for the Lord's house. If you don't have a penny, give your time and your heart, and God will bless you.

Sometimes when I Had more than one penny and I walked by myself, I would stop at the Phillips Station that was on my route to church, and I would put a penny in the gumball machine and get a big jawbreaker bubblegum. Then I would walk down the street to Sunday school at Tabernacle Missionary Church, our family church.

Momma also taught us to value school and family. She said, "You need your education: finish high school and go to college because nobody can take what you learn away from you. Love and help your family whenever they are in need; your family is your blood kin."

Chapter 3

Momma, I'm Sick

The neighbor next to our property had a cherry tree, and hanging on the branches were the most beautiful cherries, but the tree stood in the middle of a cesspool. My sisters and brothers and I were very hungry, and there was no other source of food, so we all picked up the cherries that fell in the cesspool, cleaned them with our breath, dried them with our clothes, and then ate them. I was at Dunbar School in the classroom when it all began. I became very sick. I knew the rules: I was to tell my teacher I was ill. She would then send me to the nurse's office. I took my lunch, which was in a bread sack, with me when it was time for recess. I wasn't planning on coming back to class. I took one last look at the steps that lead to the school's door; they seemed as if they were too many to climb. I decided I was going home to Momma instead. I walked to the edge of the road that led to the street. I knew to look to my left and to my right, up and down the street. There were no cars coming, so I crossed the street and went home.

I finally made it to our house, feeling worse than before. Momma was naturally surprised to see me because school had not dismissed, but she could see something was wrong.

I told her I was ill. She felt my head and told me to lie on the living room couch. She took my temperature and gave me medicine.

The medication was not working, and I was getting weaker and weaker. Momma used the neighbor's telephone to call our family doctor. When the medication the doctor prescribed didn't help me either, the doctor came to our home with his black bag. I was afraid of the heavyweight doctor. He advised Momma that I had to be hospitalized.

Walking with Momma

Momma didn't own an automobile, so we walked to AM hospital, which was very far from our home. The emergency room staff performed tests on me, and when the testing was complete, the results were terrifying. The doctors informed Momma that I was a very sick child, possibly terminally ill, but the hospital could not admit me because the disease I had was contagious. As we walked home,

Momma talked to herself the whole time. She said to me, You are not going to die!" I knew then that something was very wrong with me.

Letter for Momma

Momma received a letter from our family doctor that instructed her to bring me to SJ Hospital. Momma and I again walked to the hospital, where testing was performed, but the results were the same as before. I had a contagious disease, and the hospital could not admit me. Meanwhile, our home was under quarantine.

Our family doctor didn't give up on the situation, though. He sent Momma yet another letter advising her to bring me to St. Anthony's hospital, where I was finally admitted.

Lonely Days

Momma and I arrived at the hospital, and Sister Adeltrudis, a nun, lead me to a small room. She immediately instructed me to remove my clothing, and she gave me a pair of pajamas. She helped me to climb into the big white bed; then she pulled up the rails. This room became my home for approximately a year. No visitors were allowed in my room because of the contagious disease. My momma was allowed to peek through a tiny glass window that looked out into the hall off my room, but that was all. I was from a large family and was not used to being alone. Naturally, I was very lonely.

Sister Adeltrudis became very dear to me. She taught me how to fold my hands and pray every day. She came to my room three and four times a day, giving me breakfast, lunch, snack, and supper. She also played games with me. I had never felt love the way she demonstrated it in her kindness toward me. I shall never forget her and will always cherish her love and my memories of her. Because of her love I decided that when I grew older I was going to be Catholic like her. My best friend and I made a vow that we were both going to be Catholic, never marry, each buy a brick house, and live next door to each other until we died. I told Momma, and she smiled. Of course that never happened.

The Promise

While I was sick, I was so lonely in my room lying in my bed that I began to bite my fingernails. Sister Adeltrudis promised that if I'd quit biting my fingernails, she would give me a gift. I believed her so I stopped biting my fingernails. When I wanted to bite my fingernails, I thought about the promised gift. When the nun would come in my room for prayer, breakfast, lunch, snacks, and supper, I showed her my fingernails and informed her I hadn't bitten them. I always wanted to know where the

gift she had promised was. She would always smile and say, "Be patient. You will get your gift." She kept promising me, and I believed her. *But when?* I thought.

Peekaboo, I See You

Every now and then I'd look toward the door to see Momma's face peering through the tiny window glass. One beautiful day Momma was wearing a pretty fur coat. I told her I liked her coat. She smiled at me and said, "This coat isn't new." She began to model the coat by turning herself around and around. Then she said to me, "I'll save this coat for you when you get out of the hospital, and when you become a big girl, I'll give it to you because you like it that much." Momma also bought be a bottle of lotion and told me that it would help my hair grow again. Sister Adeltrudis had cut my hair when I arrived because of the illness.

Waving to My Brothers and Sister

It was very cold outside and snowing heavily when Sister Adeltrudis came into my room and said she had a surprise for me. I was so excited. *"What could it be?* I thought. She allowed me to go into the hallway and stand on a register, and I looked out of a window high from the ground. To my surprise, I saw my brothers and sister waving at me. They weren't allowed to come into the hospital, so they stood there waving and smiling. I waved back, thrilled because I hadn't seen them for months. Also I wasn't allowed to get out of bed for months, so this was a real treat for me. That was the only time I saw my siblings during my stay in the hospital.

Miraculous Healing

Lying in my hospital bed, heaven opened up to me. I had a vision of a great big beam of light coming down from heaven. This beam shone bright upon the earth. I heard music that sounded like legions of angelic beings singing continually throughout this vision. I saw forms of men and women running toward this beam of light. As the shadows approached the beam, it would step into the light. I was the only child there, and I was fascinated by the music. I began heading toward the beam of light, too. I wanted to hear what the angels were singing. As I got closer, I heard "O come let us adore Him," "O come let us adore Him," O come let us adore Him-mm." They held that last note before they finished the song. I awakened from the vision and was healed of the contagious disease, typhoid fever. I still thank God for the miraculous healing. I told Momma and my nurse what I saw. I thought it was reality, but they said it was a dream and that God can visit me in dreams and visions.

The Promised Gift

One day Sister Adeltrudis entered into my room and announced, "Lorena, you are going home to your family. I know you will be happy to see your brothers and sisters. Your momma is here to take you home, and I have a surprise for you." The gift was that she gave me all of the toys I had played with during my stay in the hospital. I was thrilled about all of my gifts. I soon was sad though when I realized I was leaving Sister Adeltrudis, the nun I had come to love so dearly. I knew I would probably never see her again. I waved good-bye as tears of sadness rolled down my cheeks. The last time I saw her, she was smiling as she waved good-bye. Momma and I turned as we walked down the hallway that led us out of the hospital.

Chapter 4

My First Real Fight

I was in the third grade when my brother Jerry informed me he was not going to fight any more of my battles; I had to learn to fight for myself. We were at recess playing on school property when he told me, and I knew I wasn't going to fight, but at that moment my heart started beating rapidly. Fear engulfed me. I depended on him to fight for me.

When I was in the fifth grade, a girl approached me in the hall at school. She informed me that she was going to fight me. She knew I had a reputation of allowing children to bully me. She told me she would meet me after school. Usually at this point fear would grip my heart, but this day, it did not. Instead I was relaxed; the heavy pressure of fear seemed to be released somehow. I agreed, and after school dismissal my best friend and I walked home extra slowly in case the girl still wanted to fight.

I was almost home when the girl and her pack of friends approached me. There was also a crowd waiting to egg on the fight, which began with a wood chip on my shoulder that was supposed to be knocked off by the other girl. Instead of knocking the chip off of my shoulder though, she started cursing. Then it was my turn. Someone placed a chip on her shoulder to be knocked off. Instantly I knocked the chip off of her shoulder and begin hitting her violently. For once in my life I was tired of being bullied and tired of fear. I fought her until I lost consciousness of everything around me except the fight. This was my first experience and my mind simply went blank.

At first my best friend was egging me on: "Beat her, Lorene! Beat her!" I saw blood gushing from the girl's mouth, but I continued fighting. That is when I heard my best friend shouting at me. She was crying over and over, and it sounded like she was at a distance. "Stop! You're killing her! You're killing her!"

I was at a point of no return, though, and I couldn't stop. The next thing I remember, I was being held in midair by a pair of hands grasping my clothes tightly. The hands belonged to my brother J. C. I was still fighting the air. The girl that I was fighting, the crowd, and my best friend were gone. My brother gently loosed his hands from me. As I stood up, he said, "Let's go home."

Chapter 5

Come and See Come and See

Up until I was eleven years old I lived a quiet life. I was an obedient child, and I believed everything Momma said. Momma said God saw everything we say and do.

Our family had an outhouse made of wood, and my uncle's outhouse was made of block I was afraid of both of them. I worried that the floor would cave in, and I would drown in all of that mess. So I would go behind the outhouse and squat. I would always look around to make sure nobody was watching; then I would gaze toward the sky because I knew the Lord saw everything I did. Later that day before I lay down for a nap, I asked the Lord how He could see everything we did. I fell fast asleep. I dreamed I was in heaven, where an angel was looking down a huge barrel. It said to me, "Come and see, come and see." I then noticed I had wings as the angel did, so I flew over to where the angel was. When I looked down into the big round barrel, I saw the whole world. Everything on earth looked so small: miniature cars, miniature houses, and miniature people.

I awakened and I understood how the Lord saw everything I did and said. This world is like a barrel. The Lord of heaven and earth is higher than all. He made everything and sees all things. I thank God for answering my childhood question in a dream.

Chapter 6

The Power of the Trigger: War between Two Voices

Getting out of bed early one morning, I tiptoed into the kitchen to get my share of food because food was scarce in our home. I thought everyone was sleeping until I heard Momma calling my name. "Lorene!" (That was the nickname she gave me.) "Get those dishes washed." I was very angry because I knew my sister Faye-Baby had not washed the dishes the day before when it was her turn and Momma knew it, too. She always waited on my day to make me do two days of dishes. I didn't want to do my sister's chores. Why didn't Momma have her do her own chores?

My second brother had been partying and drinking when he came home that night. Before he went to sleep, he had laid the gun on top of the old-fashioned stereo. Momma wasn't aware of this situation.

This was the first time I experienced two voices talking to me. I realized later in life that it was the voice of God and the voice of the devil. The first voice said to me, "Do you see that gun over there?" I looked and thought *yes!* "If I were you," it said, "I would take that gun and put it to my head and shoot because there're probably no bullets in it." That sounded all right. I picked up the gun and pointed it to the temple of my forehead and would have pulled the trigger, but I heard another voice speaking to me saying, "If I were you, I wouldn't do that." I then rested my arm to my side, the gun still in my hand.

Again I heard the voice speaking to me saying, "If I were you, I would take the gun and point it to my head and shoot because there're probably no bullets in it and you shouldn't have to do your sister's dishes." I again obeyed the voice that was speaking to me. As soon as I pointed the gun to my head, I heard another voice interrupt saying, "If I were you, I wouldn't do that." So I rested the gun by my side.

A third time I heard the voice speaking to me. "If I were you ..., but before it could finish speaking, the other voice interrupted, saying, You see those records over there?" The records were stacked about four feet high on the top of the stereo. I looked and in my mind, I said, "Yes" the voice said to me, If there aren't any bullets in that gun, pull the trigger and shoot those records. I remember I couldn't. I couldn't seem to move. Then a power came into my hand, and it pulled my trigger finger for me, and the gun fired! The records shattered into pieces all over the living room. Momma jumped out of bed screaming, not knowing what had happened.

Chapter 7

The Hellfire Message

Our family moved from Lincoln Avenue and relocated to Johnson Street, which is when I met my best friend, Bonny. Momma rented a house from a lady preacher and her husband. All of the children in the neighborhood attended Bible class in a house she remodeled for the occasion. Her husband loaded most of the children in his crowded station wagon and drove us there. We also attended Bible class at St John's Baptist Church. It was fun waiting in line for the big yellow church bus. I remember my teacher Ms. Favors; she taught us about our roots. I will forever remember the African song "Come by Here, Lord" and "Peanut Butter and Jelly Sandwich."

Our family attended The Church of God on Sundays. It was on a country road, and this reverend and his wife also provided rides for the neighborhood children along with their own children in his station wagon. I liked the reverend and his wife; they were kind people. Years later the church purchased property in our neighborhood, and we were able to walk to church. No more fun rides in the old station wagon. Eventually the church grew big enough to build a beautiful cathedral.

Each summer on the church's anniversary, we had an old-fashioned picnic in the rear church lot, which still held woods and the trees. Light's was placed in the trees because the picnic was from dawn to dusk. The mothers of the church invited us to eat as much as we wanted. They would raise their voices, calling out, "You kids want some more chocolate cake?" That was music to our ears, as food was scarce in our home. I would get so full that I'd feel like I would burst. These were the good old days. This church is where I got religion.

Old-time Religion at Twelve

Every Sunday morning, Reverend preached a conviction message. He preached about hellfire. I shall never forget one particular Sunday morning. My best friend, Bonny, and I hadn't planned on getting religion that day. It was the summer of 1957. She was eleven and I was twelve years old. We had to be baptized before we died because we wanted to go to heaven with Jesus. We didn't want to go to the burning furnace with the devil. Momma said when I reached twelve years old I had to give account for my own sins. Until then my sins were on her because she was responsible for me and had to answer to God for my sins. If I died before I was twelve, I would go to heaven. She said Jesus was twelve when He became responsible for His actions. I didn't care if Momma had to answer to God for my sins; I was going to heaven anyway. When I reached twelve, however, I was very much concerned about getting religion. I believed what Momma said about there being a heaven and hell and Jesus dying for my sins.

My best friend and I went to church as usual, but this day wasn't the same. The reverend preached his conviction message; it was about hellfire, and my best friend looked at me with tears pouring down her cheeks. Something touched me; I felt the tears in my eyes as I fought to keep from crying. I had a reputation of being strong, and I had to maintain it. Although my heart was convicted, I couldn't allow the tears to fall or my friends would see I wasn't strong.

The reverend asked if anyone wanted to come to the altar. My best friend nudged my shoulder, and I knew it was time. We had made a vow a while back that we would get saved together. She whispered my name softly. We walked to the altar, where some chairs stood in for the mourners' bench. My friend and I each took a chair. The reverend and church mothers dressed in white apparel touched us on our heads and shoulders, and they prayed for us in hopes that we were sincere about our religion. And so I was saved at twelve years old in a small interdenominational church.

I felt the presence of God then and have talked to Him daily. He has answered me verbally, in dreams and visions. I tried very hard to be converted; fighting and cursing were my downfalls. When I made mistakes, I asked Jesus to forgive me just like Momma said. I read the Bible faithfully, but I couldn't understand the parables. I prayed for an understanding of His Word. I want to go to heaven when I die.

Chapter 8

The Old-Fashioned Extension Cord

I was fifteen years old and life was tough living at home with Momma. I remember being very hungry. It was Momma's pay day, and she had come home from cashing her paycheck. She usually brought groceries home, but this time she didn't. She was counting her money when I asked her for fifty cents to buy a Pepsi Cola and a chocolate cake. She said she was not going to give it to me and for me to go outside to play. I was angry and informed her that she had been gone all day, and she should have brought food home. I went outside but not to play. I began yelling harsh words stating I was going to report her to the authorities because I was hungry and she was supposed to have food in the house. I would have gotten away with this statement, but the boy next door mocked my words. "Lorena, what did you say? Report her to the ABC woman, uh!" He laughed and laughed, and when Momma heard him, she was angry. (What I didn't know was that when she lived in a different state, she had left her nine-year-old child home babysitting his brothers and sister. The neighbors had reported her to the authorities, and the children were taken from the home.) When I made that accusation, it was a reminder of this incident. She called me into the house for an old-fashioned extension cord whipping. At first when she starting beating me, I was crying. She whipped me so long that I became numb, so I stopped crying. It didn't hurt anymore. That was when Momma got really angry. She tried to make me cry, so she whipped me over and over again. While she was whipping me, I was lying on the floor, and something unexplainable happened to me. I heard a voice speaking to me (I didn't realize it was the devil). It said, "If I were you, I'd jump up, hit her in the face, run out of the house, and never come back." Another voice spoke to me (I didn't know it was the voice of God). "If you do this, you know your brother Jerry can outrun you. She will tell him to catch you and bring you back in the house, and she will kill you."

While the voices were speaking to me, Momma was still whipping me. I was angry; all of a sudden a power came over me that I cannot describe, and it made me jump high in the air. Momma, who was half on me, flew off, and she went high in the air, too. When she landed on the floor, she was wide-eyed with fear and anger, and she screamed. I stood in front of her. I looked her squarely in the face and yelled at her, "I hate you! I hate you!" After hearing this she took her fist and continued to beat me until she beat me into the other room. I didn't try to fight; I just wanted to die. I just wanted her to kill me.

When she was tired of fist-fighting me, she picked up an old-fashioned cast iron and threw it at me. I ducked, and it missed me and made a giant hole in the wood door. She then came over to me again and continued to beat me with her fist into a corner of the room. All the time I never mourned or cried. I know that on that day when I was fifteen years old, I *hated* my mother! Each passing day that hate grew and grew in my heart. I obeyed her and did what was required of me, but the trust was gone.

Chapter 9

Teenage Marriage

At the age of fifteen Momma said I could "social date." This meant dating more than one boy. She said that dating one-on-one would get me in trouble, but social dating would keep me out of trouble. The first time I laid eyes on one boy in our neighborhood, it was love. I would secretly peek out of my bedroom window and watch him all of the time, hoping he would notice me. I liked the way he walked, the way he talked, the way he dressed—to me he looked like a movie star. I didn't want to date any other boys, so we began to date one-on-one, disobeying Momma's rules.

When Momma saw that I was dating only him, she started talking against him in hopes that I would discontinue dating him, but it drew me closer to him. When that didn't work, Momma accused me of doing things I was taught not to do. At first I would cry because it hurt that she didn't trust me. I had plans for graduating, becoming employed, moving into my own house, getting married, and birthing lots of children so I could love them. As time flew by and I turned sixteen, I started doing what she accused me of. Then when she started accusing me of unfaithfulness, I would secretly laugh. By and by my sins caught up with me, and I became pregnant. We decided to get married. My wedding gown consisted of a two-piece blue maternity outfit. Momma pleaded for me not to marry and said that our marriage would not survive. Our marriage survived twelve years and five sons, but in the end, Momma was right.

Chapter 10

The Great Experience

I became a true worshipper of Jesus Christ in the family of God at the Church of God in Christ when I was twenty-eight years old. In this church I became the director of the Sunshine Band, which is a children's choir and teaching session group. I remember the first song God allowed the holy angels to sing to me in a dream: "Bring the Backsliders on Home." He gave me many musical songs and hymns of praise in dreams in my hour of trials and disappointments. He informed me I would record albums, and I believe the Spirit of God.

God has done so much for me that I can never repay all He has done. I welcome Him to receive the glory from my life and to do according to His purpose. I thank God for this great experience in Him. I received the baptism of the Holy Spirit and experienced the love of God. I was healed and delivered of the hurtful experiences in my life. I began to love my mother, and I thank God He put forgiveness in my heart for her. My relationship with her has changed so much that I was actually able to kiss her. I hadn't kissed her even as a young child. As the tears rolled down her cheeks, I knew she knew I had forgiven her. With Jesus in your heart it makes it so much easier to say "I'm sorry."

God did the same for me with my husband. God healed and delivered me from the bitterness, depression, and anger that lingered in my heart against him.

The Spirit of God Speaks

Another amazing experience from God happened before Momma became ill. The Spirit of God spoke to me, saying that He was going to take my momma to her spiritual home. I prayed and asked God in His son Jesus's name to give some of my life to Momma. I was not ready for her to go to her eternal home. Many times when I drove down the highway, I would see an older women walking. The Spirit of God would remind me that that could be my mother walking and that one day I would not see her because she would be no more. I would become nervous and pray harder.

One day I was driving in the downtown area around the department stores when I saw a lady exiting the bi-state bus. My momma and this lady were look-alikes. I soon discovered it was her sister, Aunt Louise. The Spirit of God said to me, "When I take your mother home, you will have your aunt."

Chapter 11

If Only I Had Known the Truth

One day I decided to take a journey to find my father. My friend and I drove to Lima, Ohio, where my brother said my father and mother lived when I was conceived. He also gave me an address to try. My friend and I arrived in the city, and we lodged at the nearest hotel. In the morning we drove to my uncle's house but we didn't enter the home; instead we went through the neighborhood ringing doorbells, hoping we would find older people that knew about my dad. We ended up going in circles though, always ending at my dad's house. With no results we drove back to our hometown.

I telephoned Momma, and somehow she knew where I'd been. She said, "Your trip was in Lima, wasn't it?" I answered, "Yes!" She then asked me whether I'd found my father. I told her no, but that Uncle Jeep really got on my nerves. He wanted me to be around him all of the time, and he kept hugging me. "The next time I go to Lima, I'm not going to his house," I told her. Momma laughed and giggled, and I didn't understand what was so funny. Little did I know her thoughts about the irony of the situation. As a child I had often said how much I loved my father and that I wanted to live with him, yet when finally I met him, I didn't know who he was, said that I didn't like him hugging me, and said I wasn't going back to his house.

I wrote a letter to my uncle asking him if he knew who my father was. My older brother had said he would know. I received an astonishing letter in the mailbox. These words were underlined, and it took me years to put the puzzle together. *I can't see how I'm your father, I do love you, yours forever.* In his own way, he told me he was my father. Reading these words from the last sentence to the first, it reads: yours forever, I do love you, I'm your father, I don't know how.

One day I telephoned uncle continually asking him about my father until it vexed him. He said to me, You were born a Goodman, and you will die a Goodman." I didn't understand that statement. *I am who I am because I carry my momma's married name*, I thought. When Uncle spoke these words, a vision of a photo flashed before my eyes. I remembered when I was in the seventh grade and school photos were taken individually of each student, I asked Momma why did I have my eyes bulked and told her that the picture was ugly. Momma laughed but didn't answer me. The image of my uncle also flashed before me. In that photo, the resemblance was clear. I heard the Spirit of God speaking to me saying, "He is your father." My uncle and my father are the same.

If only I had known the truth. One day when Momma was grooming my hair, I began speaking to her. "Now I know why I was being punished most of my life; you were not beating me, you were beating my father." She said to me, The good Lord will tell you who your father is." I told her I understood but didn't reveal to her that I already knew. She couldn't deal with the facts.

Now I Know

One March day at 10 a.m. while working on my job, my spirit suddenly cried loudly, *Lord, I don't want to go home!* I didn't understand this outburst, but I knew something wasn't right at home. Later I telephoned Momma's home because I knew she planned to pick up her great-granddaughter from my home, and I knew she was true to her word. I didn't receive an answer. At 4 p.m. I rushed home from work knowing something had happened to Momma. When I pulled into the driveway, I saw my third son playing basketball, which was why he hadn't answered the telephone. I asked him if he had heard from Momma, and he said he hadn't. By this time, I was beginning to shake, fear grasping my heart. I telephoned Momma's home—no answer. Was she hurt? I hung up the telephone planning to go to her home when the phone rang. It was a nurse from the hospital stating that Momma was sick. She had gained consciousness and was able to tell the nurse her daughter's name and where she worked. They had called there first, but it was right after I'd left. I learned later that Momma was on the bi-state bus when she became very sick. She'd asked the bus driver to stop the bus so she could get off. She thought she could walk the sickness off as before, but instead she fainted. Somebody saw her and called the ambulance (thank you, Jesus), and Momma was transferred to St. Louis University Hospital. The surgeon there said she'd suffered an aneurysm.

As I walked into her hospital room, she said to me, "Be quiet, I'm praying I'm in heaven." Then she looked at me and called me by her bedside. She had always told me that when she knew she was going to die she would tell me who my father was. I knew what she was going to say. I told her I didn't want to know, but she was true to her word, her promise. She said "Lorene, Vernon." I pretend I didn't hear her, but she repeated it again. Momma survived the aneurysm two weeks. One week before she passed she saw her destination. March 31, 1987, she said, "I'm in heaven." God gave us one glorious year to be together after I prayed and asked him to give Momma some of my life. Amen

Chapter 12

Testimonies

Prophecy

I visited a church to hear the testimony of a traveling evangelist, who at the age of seven was playing with a metal hanger and accidentally caught the hanger in his eye. He pulled the hanger out of his eye, and the fluid poured out, making him blind. Surgeons operated to replace his eye with a glass eye. After receiving prayer he was miraculously healed and could see out of the socket of the blind eye. As he demonstrated his testimony, the ushers were preparing to receive donations for the evangelist. I knew I only had a dollar in my purse. I didn't have any money anywhere. So I folded the dollar in the palm of my hand and prayed a faith prayer. I said, "Lord, this man of God is a full-time evangelist. He has a wife and a daughter, and I really want to support this ministry." I looked at the folded dollar in my hands and said, "Lord, bless this dollar in the name of Jesus, and let it be a blessing to this family. And if I had more, I would give it to this man of God's ministry." I walked to the offering basket lying on a table and put the dollar in. As I lifted my hand from the basket, the evangelist caught my hand and immediately began to prophesy. He said to me, "God said you are a songwriter, and you will be recording and singing with the anointing he has given you because God has given you a double anointing." He said he could see in the Spirit people talking against what God has given me, but he could also see me continually prospering in the Lord. Then he could see the people looking on in amazement.

My Life Flashing before My Eyes

I was depressed while expecting my fifth child because my husband and I lived in separate houses. I was in labor and my husband was driving me to the hospital. We were arguing the entire trip because he didn't want to drive me. I was in great pain and it was raining heavily. I wanted to tell him to stop the car so I could walk to the hospital, but the labor pains were so forceful, I knew my baby and I would not survive. I was nearly ecstatic with relief when we arrived at the hospital. My husband informed me he had to move the car from the emergency parking space. He assured me he would be back. That was the last time I saw him that day. As I was laboring with child, my pains ceased as my life flashed before me. I knew I was going to die, and I wanted to die. I felt life was not worth living. I talked to Jesus and said, "Lord, I am ready to die if you are ready for me." I wasn't worried about my children because I knew He was going to take care of them. At that instance the doctor discovered the problem, and Jesus and I delivered an eight-pound-eleven-ounce beautiful baby boy. I gave him a biblical name, Aaron, meaning "exalted." He shall be great in the sight of the Lord.

Not Lucky, Just Blessed by Jesus

I am not ashamed of the gospel of Jesus Christ or the gifts God has given me. Or what He has called and chosen for me to do. On October 23, 1998, I was driving on Rock Springs Drive. On my way to the nail technician and then on to church, I stopped at a stop sign. After looking right and left on College Avenue and seeing no headlights or vehicles, I proceeded to make my right turn when the accident occurred. I immediately prayed for God's protection as the automobile rolled over and over. I heard the voice of the devil speaking to me, saying I was going to die. My life flashed before my eyes as each of my five sons appeared before me. I prayed to Jesus for each child, to make them strong and to not grieve long. Each of my grandchildren also appeared before me. I prayed that Jesus would take care of them, as I knew He would, because I knew I would no longer be on this earth for them.

I spoke to Jesus and said, "Jesus, I can't stop the car." That's when He gave me instructions on what to do. By obeying God, the car stopped rolling. Then it felt like two iron hands on each side of my head crushing it. I said out loud, "I know I'm saved, but I don't want to go through this." I heard my name being called. I was pondering over the name, thinking, *Did I hear Lorene or Lorena? Did I hear my name correctly?* The next thing I knew I was lying on my back in a place of peace. My being was made up of peace; my surroundings were peace. The whole atmosphere was peace. I could hear, though I had no ears; I could see, but had no eyes; I could talk, but had no mouth. I had no body, yet I was lying on my back. Then I heard a voice speaking to me. I turned my head toward the voice, and it said to me, "You are going to die." I looked and I saw a barrier. I knew I was going to my final destination—eternal life. I said to the voice, "I know." I was aware that it was the voice of the devil, but I had no fear, for perfect love casts out all fear. I turned my head the other direction. I began to talk to Jesus. I said, It looks like you are going to have to get somebody else to finish the ministry." Then I turned my head up straight. At that moment Jesus spoke to me and said, "All things I said you should do in ministries you will do. You will not die. It shall come to pass. I turned to position my head up straight. I don't know how long it was when I started fading, fading. I heard someone calling out; it seems like miles away. Are you hurt in there? I could not talk because I had not yet faded back into my body. When I came back into my body, my right hand was on the steering wheel my left hand was by my side in the door. I had two broken fingers, but my body was not sore, and I had no concussion. A melody from a Christian album was playing.

Not lucky, but blessed by Jesus. I am sold out to God and covered with His blood. The devil can't do me any harm.

Healed of Asthma

When I became an adult, I developed asthma. I was traveling to and fro to the hospital for shots to help manage it. One day I was dressed to attend a Wednesday night Bible class, but first I was planning on going to the hospital to get a shot. Suddenly I heard the voice of God speaking to me saying, "What do you want to do? Do you want to go to the hospital and get a shot? Or do you want to go to church tonight and get delivered of asthma?" I decided to trust in God and go to church to get healed. I picked my spiritual mom up, and we drove to the department store to get some undergarments because I was too ill to wash my clothes. I thought, *If I die, I'm going to die with clean undergarments.*

As we entered the church, my breathing was worse. I was gasping for air. The pastor of the church asked me to come to the altar to receive prayer. He instructed the congregation to get on their knees and pray with him. As the people prayed, my breathing was barely a gasp. I heard the voice of the devil speaking: "You should have gone to the hospital to get that shot; now you are going to die." As we walked around and around the aisle, I kept trying to go outside for air, but the sisters of the church would not let me. In my mind I said to the devil, "If I die, I am going to heaven, and you won't have a chance to get me." As quickly as my mind said those words, I took my last gasp and began breathing normally. At that moment I was healed from asthma. Thank you, Jesus!

Chapter 13

Dreams

The Angelic Messenger

I dreamed an angel came from heaven. As I looked in the sky, I saw him standing in midair. Crowds of people were outside standing and talking to each other, but their conversation stopped as they gazed upon the angel in midair. The angel asked a question: "Who will go? Who will go?" My thoughts were that I wanted to go, but I waited on the crowd's response. No one opened their mouths, so I spoke and said, "I will go!" Then I noticed I had wings, and I followed the angel as we flew all over the world. The angel then brought me back where I was before he took me around the world. I didn't want to come back; I wanted to fly into heaven. I looked up at the angel who was still in midair. I asked him a question: "What would keep me out of heaven? He replied, "Those songs." He was referring to the recordings the angels had sung to me when I was going through my tests and trials. He continued speaking: "Those songs are anointed and they are to go all over the world, so souls may be saved." I was surprised at his answer because I knew my sins were forgiven. I thought the angel would say "Nothing."

I awakened from the dream disturbed, and I cried out to God and said, "God, in Jesus's name, what am I going to do? I have no money to record these songs. I've done all I know to do." Not many days after I talked to Jesus I talked to a friend about the situation. I told her I had to find a musician and a studio. She came to my rescue, and I was interviewed about a month later. God blessed me with a way to record my first album in 1994. I asked Jesus what to name the album. He said, "Lorena Burnett & The Gift of God Ministries: Nobody but You, Lord" All of these songs are a gift from heaven; they are not of my own invention.

After the recording was released, a co-worker said, "Lorena, you need to go into the community. Who is going to buy your album if it doesn't get publicity?" I said to her, "I am going to go by the recipe of God and His instructions." I really had no clue how the songs were going to get publicity, but I knew the Lord was going to make a way.

Heaven a Dream

I dreamed I was in heaven. There were crowds of people there, and everybody was happy. The heavenly atmosphere was peaceful and beautiful There were dimensions in heaven. I dreamed a friend, Joe Anna, was there. I've known her since we were children on earth, and we were so happy to see each other; we laughed and talked. There was no end to this world.

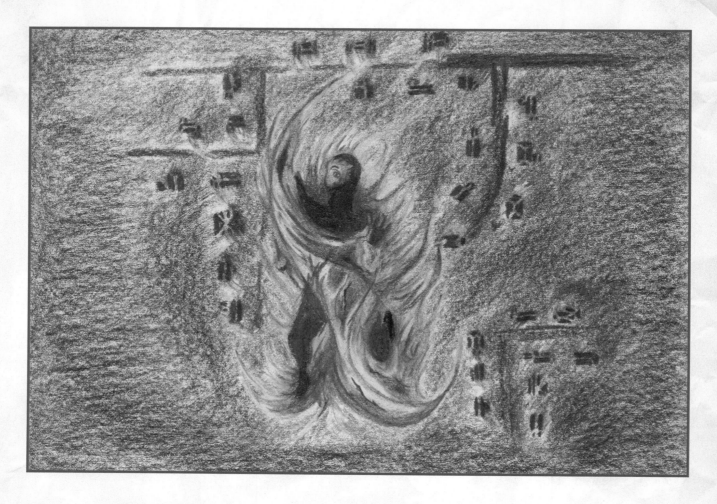

The Burning Ball of Flame

I dreamed I fell backward from the sky. I screamed, "Oh no!" but it was too late. I landed on the ground and became a ball of fire. I was not alone: every person on earth was a great big ball of fire. I knew I was trapped and there was no way out of this situation without Jesus in my life. Trapped in my own sins, lost forever, separated from God, I realized all of my chances for forgiveness were gone. I remembered my life on earth and all the deeds I had done. I was doomed forever in my private furnace, burning in my own flames.

Chapter 14

Visions

The Demon

My children and I attended a church revival service that was conducted by a prophet, a minister anointed and appointed by God. He began to pray the dismissal prayer but was interrupted by the voice of God. He said the voice advised him to tell the congregation that if the devil appeared to any one of us, we should plead the blood of Jesus. I drove home from church feeling renewed and refreshed in the Spirit of God. I usually brewed tea, but this particular night I went straight to my bedroom to relax and ponder over the wonderful service.

The children were in the next bedroom playing. I could hear them laughing. As I glanced toward my doorway, my body became numb, frozen in shock at what I saw, My eyes beheld a thing I shall never forget, a big black round head. Its eyes were flames of fire; its nose and mouth were all flames of fire. It did not have a body. As I was gazing at the demon, I tried to get out of bed, but I couldn't. I tried to call out to my children, but I was speechless. The demon that was in midair moved toward me as I lay frozen in my bed and engulfed me. Its head covered my head, and it continued choking me. Over and over, in my mind I prayed *Jesus, Jesus, Jesus.* Then I remembered the words of the prophet saying the Lord had told him to tell us that if the devil appeared, we should plead the blood of Jesus. I did as I was instructed. Immediately, like an explosion, I heard a popping sound, and the demon vanished in midair. I was able to get out of bed.

Zorias—I'm Coming in a Mighty Way

One day while working at my job, I had an open vision. I saw a three-foot-tall man and was amazed at his appearance and was staring at him. I asked him, "What is your name?" He answered boldly, "My name is Zo-ri-as, and I'm coming in a mighty way." Pointing at him with the index finger of my right hand, I said in a commanding voice, "There is nothing you can do to me. I am saved and sanctified, filled with the Holy Ghost and sold out to Jesus." Then I looked in the background and saw a host of three-foot-tall men. They had helmets on their heads, and stripes of red blood were streaming from their helmets. They carried swords by their sides, and they were riding white horses swiftly as if they were riding to battle, though their legs were too short for their feet to reach the stirrups. I said to Zorias, "There is nothing you or all your imps can do to me. I am saved, sanctified, and filled with the Holy Ghost." Then I began to laugh over and over again. When I came out of the vision, I was still standing at my job laughing.

Chapter 15

Prayers

Jesus, My Divine Connection

Jesus, you are my divine connection. You're in the marrow of my bones.

You are my head and neck—connecting my whole body, controlling my hands, legs, and feet, thinking for me on my behalf.

Jesus, you are my bread, and I am so thankful for the crust in which lies all of the nutrition I need to be sustained in this life.

Jesus, you are that light that shines in my life so bright. Without your light, I would be in darkness, blacker than the depths of midnight.

I am so thankful for your guidance; with it I can choose the right path.

I am so thankful for your protection; without it I cannot weather the storms of this life.

They say trusting in something you cannot see is foolish. But I say trusting is believing. Now faith is the substance of things hoped for, the evidence of things not seen. It sees what the eye cannot see, for the mind is conscious and the vision is formed.

Faith is what touches your heart, and I desire your heart mingling with my heart. I come forth from you like a newborn baby comes forth from its mother's womb. You cut the umbilical cord. Now I am independent, yet depending on you.

In love, yes! I am deeply in love with you. As deeply as a mother who finds joy in her firstborn. And I know you love me, too. As a shepherd sacrifices himself for his lamb. You stood in my place.

You chose to take the abuse, the cursing, the whipping; with swollen lip and bowed head you asked for forgiveness on my behalf. Through great pain and sulfuring and love you felt the sting of death, and you gave up the ghost. From the depths of hell, you remember the cutting of the umbilical cord. That was me because of that divine connection. Jesus, you rose from the dead to set a sinner like me *free*.

Expression of Gratitude

Jesus, it's so good to live the life you have given me. You are that life—the light that shines in places that seem so dark.

It is so pleasant to have someone who never gets bored of listening to my everyday chatter.

You mold me; you understand me better than I understand myself.

I have come to grips with myself, knowing I'm different. I thank you for giving me another family, those that are spiritual.

They understand my dreams and visions. I feel like I am in another galaxy, though in reality I am here in this world.

The minutes, hours, days, weeks, months, and years are hanging over me. What have I accomplished in this life?

These ministries you have placed inside of me: have they brought souls into your kingdom?

Is this life I am now living for naught? When the sleet, hail, storms, and hurricanes of this life come, stay with me; don't you ever leave me, not even for a moment. —Your Daughter.

In Closing

I wrote this book about my life story to the glory and honor of God. I pray you will experience the presence of God and be blessed as you read my life story. There are wounded and hurting people of this world who have been through torments in life as I have. There are many unanswered questions. Our Father, which art in heaven, has all your answers, and *He* knows how to put the puzzle of your life together.

I have more questions, even now. God help me to understand my sister Faye-Baby and myself. She asked me a question: she wanted to know why I didn't like her when we were children. I didn't know. I told her she was a tomboy, and as a child I disliked that about her. When writing my life story though, I discovered the truth. When I was quite young, Momma planted seeds of dislike in my heart for my sister by giving her the things I had picked for myself: the Lila Lou doll and the red dress, for example. Also hurtful was being punished for rock throwing though my sister was not punished and being made to do her chores on top of mine. As the seeds were watered by those deeds, hardness against her grew in my heart.

Nevertheless I truly love my parents; they will forever be in my dreams and heart. These words will forever stay in my mind as well. Momma said to me, "I trust you, but I ask one thing: look after your sister Faye-Baby." I am a living testimony of what God can and will do in you and through you. First put your faith, trust, and hope in Jesus because love is just like Him. When all is said and done, *Nobody but You, Lord* makes me feel the way I do. Amen.

A Note about Sr. Adeltrudis

Personal Speculation of FR. Damien R. Doughtery, O.F.M. Regarding
Sister M. Adeltrudis Neufeld, F.S.G.M. Franciscan Religion
March 28, 1923–May, 7, 2004

One time as our Holy Father St. Francis was inspiring his earliest companions with confidence, he said, "Dearest Brothers, let us consider our vocation. God in his mercy, called us not merely for our own salvation but also that of many other people. Therefore, let us go through the world ..." (Leggenda dei tre compagni, Fonte Francescane, 1440)

As we perforce, find ourselves in a quiet reflective mood on the occasion of the passing of our Sister Adeltrudis, I submit that, true to our Franciscan roots and our centuries, Old tradition of respect for each person's singularity, we would do well to dwell upon her life in an attempt to glean what the prism of Sister Adeltrudis reflects of her particular realization of the almost infinite possibilities of an individual's relationship with God.

In line with Francis' exhortation, she certainly did "go through the world," from Russia to Germany to the United States and in that faith pilgrimage, multiplied her Franciscan witness to the gospel three times over as her "example and words" could testify to the people she met in Russia, Germany, and English.

AT the risk of appearing reckless and disrespectful I would like to offer my own personal speculation regarding what I perceive are traces of the heavenly Father's finger in her life so as to form her into a Franciscan Religion I do so humbly as I recognize that, while I've been familiar with her quite some time, it has only been since I moved to Alton that I had the privilege of knowing her more confidentially and learning her life's story from that lady herself.

It strikes me, powerfully, that we may actually be able to discern the Father's care and plan for SR. Adeltrudis already in her youth when she was confronted with the harshest realities of World War II and the loss of her parents, exile, and separation from her siblings. Such horror she shared with many of our Sisters who endured the suffering of that war while living in Germany. Yet, ironically or, rather, providentially, those very atrocities led her from atheism to her Catholic Faith and, ultimately, to her discovery of her Franciscan Vocation.

My personal deliberation prompted me further, however, and, perhaps, into worse foolhardiness as I asked myself if the divine design for SR. Adeltrudis' particular ministry in health care was being served through that in anguish, heartache, and deprivation she bore. I have quoted him before on this score, but William Butler Yeats' poetry is pertinent: "Too long a sacrifice can make a stone of the heart, O, when may it suffice?"

It was thanks to that very gift of faith that transformed the convulsive grief of her turbulent youth into something and someone beautiful for God. Grace preserved SR Adeltrudis from retreating into a rocky fortress of isolation of safeguard herself against further torment and, instead, motivated her, through Holy obedience, into a profession that would guarantee her being thrust into the midst of people's lives and the possibilities of attempting to alleviate pain so that others would not have to suffer alone as she had experienced.

These past several days I have heard the anecdotes recounted by you of her legendary compassion:

- Her most energetic and care of the sick and the elderly;

- Her particular solicitude for the dying and their families manifested by her non-stop vigils at their bedsides;

-Her intercessory prayers for her patients from time to time, produced such dramatic results that most skeptical of people, would not wonder;

-Her insistence upon making the Communion rounds each morning so as to spend more time with our Eucharistic Lord and, so, have more time to pray for the salvation of her family.

But the most telling illustration of SR. Adeltrudis' appreciation of ST. Francis' insistence on "example more than words" only came to light this past week through the strangest of coincidence when a former patient of more than a half- century ago decided, right at this time, to ask about her after more than fifty years.

The lady in question, Ms. Lorena Burnett, had been diagnosed in 1953 with a most contagious and, at that time, fatal disease. Not only was her home quarantined but also it appeared that she would die in total isolation and abandoned as several hospital refused to admit this eight-year-old girl. The Sisters of ST. Francis of the Martyr ST. George did welcome her, however and she was taken into St. Anthony's.

Even so, her mom a nun SR Adeltrudis came near the child

Who, for approximately a year, was the sole human contact the eight year old child would have in that bleak segregation of isolation. Ms. Burnett had many stories to narrate of the gentle, warm, loving care she received from SR. Adeltrudis but I'd like to sum them all up with the conclusions Lorena made herself when she told me: "She showed me love. She put the love of God in my heart at eight years old when nobody would care for me.

Back in February, when the regular confessor was away and for sometime after, prior to her transfer to Mother of Good Counsel Residence, SR. Adeltrudis and I would have very regular, private visits and, I must say, that each call to her room was an exact reproduction, a replay of every conversation – except for our last session.

Oh, yes we admire the work of St. Faustina and her promotion of the need for the faith in divine mercy. Sister's talk would eventually include our Blessed Mother, Our Lady of the Snows, and then, inevitably, I would admire the photographs displayed of her family and listen once again to their terrible plight. But, during that last visit, our parting was different only now, do I realize what or who prompted me to say something to put that great soul at peace regarding her family's ultimate destiny.

"Yes, Sr. Adeltrudis, but they are all waiting for you and planning a wonderful party for you when you come home. And won't it be the grandest of reunions?" She stared at me intently for some time and, only then, broke into that very individual smile of hers. You'll remember it: her eyes were so narrow, naturally, when she grinned broadly, they closed into very fine slits. She replied ever so slowly, softly but distinctly, "Yes, Yes." AMEN

Fr. Damien R. Doughtery, O.F.M.
Alton, IL 62002

12, May 2004

About the Author

Lorena Goodman Burnett was born in the town of Metropolis, Illinois. She is a divorcee and the mother of five sons. She has three sisters and seven brothers. When Lorena was young, her mom relocated to Alton, Illinois, where she attended schools and worked at Olin Corporation from 1976 to 2008. She is an ordained Evangelist and recording artist, poet, and dreamer, and has the gift of prophecy. Her hobbies are writing and singing. Her interests include traveling and exploring new places. Her desire is to own a Lila Lou doll.

lbgogmin@hotmail.com
P. O. Box 493
East Alton, IL 62024

Future Books by Lorena Burnett

Just Tools Used by God
I'm Unique (soundtrack)
Three Bs: Ben, Benita & Buster
Iish, Fish, & Wiggley Worm (soundtrack)
Fat Stuff
Booster Duck of Barstow Peak
The Conveying in the Laundry Room
Madame Butter Bean
My Dad and I

Printed in the United States
by Baker & Taylor Publisher Services